The Plains Indians

A Critical Bibliography

E. ADAMSON HOEBEL

Published for the Newberry Library

Indiana University Press

BLOOMINGTON

Published in Canada by Fitzhenry & Whiteside Limited, Don Mills Ontario

Manufactured in the United States of America

Library of Congress Cataloging in Publication Data
Hoebel, Edward Adamson, 1906-
The Plains Indians.
(Bibliographical series)
Bibliography: p.
Includes index.
1. Indians of North America--Great Plains--
Bibliography. I. Title. II. Series.
Z1209.2.G7H64   [E78.G73] 978'.004'97 77-6914
ISBN 0-253-34509-X 2 3 4 5 6 7 8 83 82

CONTENTS

The Editor to the Reader   vii

Author's Preface   1

Recommended Works   4

Bibliographical Essay

    General Introduction to the Plains Indians   6

    The Plains Area   7

    Prehistory   12

    Early Historical Contacts   14

    Tribal Cultures

        Village Tribes of the Missouri Basin   18

        Mandan   19

        Hidatsa   20

        Arikara   21

        Omaha   22

        Osage   22

        Ponca   23

        Iowa and Oto   24

        Pawnee   24

        The Nomadic Tribes   26

        Arapaho   27

Cheyenne 28

Gros Ventre (Atsina) 30

Crow 31

Teton Dakota (Lakota Sioux) 33

Blackfoot (also Blackfeet, including the Piegan) 37

Assiniboine 39

Plains Cree 40

Kiowa 41

Kiowa-Apache 43

Comanche 44

Alphabetical List and Index 46

THE EDITOR TO THE READER

A massive literature exists for the history and culture of American Indians, but the quality of that literature is very uneven. At its best it compares well with the finest scholarship and most interesting reading to be found anywhere. At its worst it may take the form of malicious fabrication. Sometimes, well-intentioned writers give false impressions of reality either because of their own limitations of mind or because they lack adequate information. The consequence is a kind of chaos through which advanced scholars as well as new students must warily pick their way. It is, after all, a history of hundreds, if not thousands, of human communities spread over an entire continent and enduring through millennia of pre-Columbian years as well as the five centuries that Europeans have documented since 1492. That is not a small amount of history.

Often, however, historians have been so concerned with the affairs of European colonies or the United States that they have almost omitted Indians from their own history. There is a way of writing "frontier history" and the "history of Indian-White relations" that often focuses so narrowly upon the intentions and desires of Euro-Americans as to treat Native Americans as though they were merely natural parts of the landscape, like forests or mountains or wild animals — obstacles to "progress" or "civilization." One of the major purposes of the Newberry Library's Center for the History of the American

Indian is to modify that narrow conception; to put Indians properly back into the central role in their own history and into the history of the United States of America as well — as participants in, rather than obstacles to, the creation of American society and culture.

The series of bibliographies of which this book is one part is intended as a guide to reliable sources and studies in particular fields of the general literature. Some of these are devoted to culture areas; others treat selected individual tribes; and a third group speaks to significant contemporary and historical issues.

The present book makes plain the difference between the way scholars classify peoples and the ways those peoples classify themselves. Although anthropologists and geographers agree that the Great Plains form a distinctive habitat and culture area, the Indians of that region conceived themselves as members of their individual tribes. Dr. Hoebel has reviewed the literature in both its regional and its tribal aspects. A special problem with regard to Plains Indians history is its identification with the familiar horse culture popularized in "cowboys and Indians" movies and romances. A special merit of Dr. Hoebel's essay is that it places the horse culture in its proper sequence as only one phase of Plains Indians history.

This work is designed in a format, standard for the series, intended to be useful to both beginning students and advanced scholars. It has two main parts: the essay (conveniently organized by subheadings) and an alphabetical list of all works cited. All citations in the essay are directly keyed, by means of bracketed numbers, to the more complete publication data in the list; and each item in the list carries a cross-reference to the page number where it is mentioned in the essay. In addition, the series incorporates several information-at-a-glance features. Among them are two sets of recommended titles: a list of five works recommended for the beginner and a group of volumes that constitute a basic library collection in the field. The large, complete list also uses asterisks to denote works suitable for secondary school students. This apparatus has been built in because the bibliographical essay, in a form familiar to scholars, could prove fairly hard going for beginners, who may wish to put it aside until they have gained sufficient background from introductory materials. Such students should come back to the essay eventually, however, because it surveys a vast sweep of information about a great variety of persons, places, communities, and events.

There is variety also in the kinds of sources because these critical bibliographies support the study of ethnohistory. Unlike older, more narrow disciplines, ethnohistory embraces the entire culture of a people; it demands contributions from a wide range of source materials. Not the least of these in the history of American Indians are their own music, crafts, linguistics, and oral traditions. Whenever possible, the authors have included such sources as well as those associated with politics, economics, geography, and so on. It will be recognized that the variety of relevant sources will change with the nature of the topic discussed.

In the last analysis this work, like all other bibliographical devices, is a tool. Each author is an expert who knows the literature and advises what source is most helpful for which purpose, but students must use this help according to their individual purposes and capacities. Many ways suggest themselves. The decision is the reader's own.

AUTHOR'S PREFACE

When most people think of the American Indian, a stereotyped vision of the painted and feather-bedecked Plains Indian warrior on horseback flashes to mind. Hollywood and white American children playing cowboys and Indians perpetuate this image. The tribes of the Plains have been the subject of fascinated attention for well over a hundred years, in Europe as well as in the United States. Not including countless novels and short stories in which Plains Indians figure prominently, some five thousand serious books, monographs, and articles have been published on Plains Indian history and cultures. They are all listed in volume 5 of George Peter Murdock and Timothy J. O'Leary's *Ethnographic Bibliography of North America* [140]. The Murdock and O'Leary bibliography is intended for the professional scholar, and as such it is indispensable. However, the student or layman who wants to learn about Plains Indians will find it bewildering in that the only clues to the contents of the works it lists are in their titles. How does one tell where to begin? How does one know which authors are the best on any given subject?

It is the intent of this bibliographical essay to help the reader find answers to such questions and not only to provide an overview of the basic, reliable literature on the Plains area and its tribes, but also to introduce the reader to current historical and anthropological knowledge concerning the origins and cultures of the major tribal peoples of the area.

In its organization, this narrative bibliography first presents the concept of the Plains as a natural and cultural area. References to the major contributions of those writers who have shaped and refined the definition of the area are introduced and assessed. Next, the basic references on the prehistoric archeology of the Plains peoples are dealt with; they show that the prehistoric population of the Plains was begun 14,000 years ago by wandering big-game hunters; they also demonstrate that agriculture as a sedentary way of life was introduced into the Plains from the east more than a thousand years ago. Following the section of prehistory, the historical accounts of fur traders and explorers who first brought European contact to the tribes of the plains are introduced. Also covered in the section on historical contact are the major sources that give the details of how Plains Indian cultures were transformed and briefly flourished after the introduction of the horse, the gun, and the fur trade with Europeans and Americans. Great tribal migrations were set in motion; the ancient populations of the settled agricultural villagers of the Missouri Basin were quickly destroyed by smallpox and the deadly depredations of invading Sioux from the east. For a brief century and a quarter, the new culture of horse-mounted bison hunters and warriors was in the ascendency until it in turn was overwhelmed by the tidal wave of white migrants in its westward sweep.

The final narrative section in this booklet then identifies and evaluates the major reliable sources on the origin and culture of each tribe that inhabited the Plains area in the nineteenth century. Although it would have been possible to order the tribes in simple alphabetical sequence, I have chosen a more dynamic, if less convenient method. The sedentary, agricultural village tribes are presented first because they represented the high climax of the pre-European mode of life on the Plains. Their cultural influence was felt by all the later tribes who entered the Plains after the introduction of the horse and gun.

In the subsection on the nomadic hunters, the tribes are presented in order of their arrival on the Plains and their ultimate degree of proximity to the old cultural focus represented by the village tribes of the Middle Missouri Basin.

Thus I hope that the reader may gain a systematic sense of the dynamic influence of historical and cultural forces in the swirling movement and emergence of new life-ways among the Plains Indians — a better sense of their interdependence and distinctive tribal identities.

As a final note, let me mention that only published works that are reasonably accessible in good libraries have been included in the bibliography. Unpublished manuscripts and archival materials, though often rich and valuable, have not been included. Nor have unpublished theses been included, though some very good ones are generally available on microfilm. They lie beyond the intended scope of this guide to literature on the Plains Indian.

RECOMMENDED WORKS

For the Beginner

[1]   Baird, W. David, *The Osage People*.

[15]   Cash, Joseph H., *The Sioux People (Rosebud)*.

[61]   Hoebel, E. Adamson, *The Cheyennes*.

[62]   Holder, Preston, *The Hoe and the Horse on the Plains*.

[111]   Lowie, Robert H., *Indians of the Plains*.

For a Basic Library

[16]   Catlin, George, *O-Kee-Pa*.

[22]   Denig, Edwin Thompson, *Five Indian Tribes of the Upper Missouri*.

[25]   Dodge, Richard Irving, *The Plains of the Great West and Their Inhabitants*.

[40]   Fletcher, Alice C., and Francis La Flesche, *The Omaha Tribe*.

[48]   Grinnell, George Bird, *The Cheyenne Indians*.

[64]   Hyde, George E., *Red Cloud's Folk*.

[109]   Lowie, Robert H., *The Crow Indians*.

[111] Lowie, Robert H., *Indians of the Plains*.

[121] MacGregor, Gordon, *Warriors without Weapons*.

[122] Mails, Thomas E., *The Mystic Warriors of the Plains*.

[126] Marriott, Alice L., *The Ten Grandmothers*.

[138] Mooney, James, *The Ghost Dance Religion and the Sioux Outbreak of 1890*.

[152] Robinson, Doane, *A History of the Dakota or Sioux Indians*.

[182] Wallace, Ernest, and E. Adamson Hoebel, *The Comanches*.

[185] Wedel, Waldo R., *Prehistoric Man on the Great Plains*.

BIBLIOGRAPHICAL ESSAY

General Introduction to the Plains Indians

Robert H. Lowie's *Indians of the Plains* [111] is the one basic book on the subject written in the English language. First published in 1954 as a Handbook of the American Museum of Natural History, it is brief, simple, and authoritative. As an introduction to Plains Indians there is none better. A more recent work (1972), profusely illustrated with dozens of fine line drawings and a number of full-color plates of paintings of Plains Indians by its author is Thomas E. Mails's *Mystic Warriors of the Plains* [122]. This lavish volume, though valuable for its illustrations, is uneven and fragmentary in its descriptions of Plains customs and usages and conveys little of the distinctive character of any one Plains Indian tribal culture as contrasted to others.

Paradoxically, serious popular interest in the Plains Indians has, it seems, consistently been stronger in Germany and Central Europe than in North America. Hence it is perhaps not too surprising that Dr. Horst Hartman's recently published *Die Plains- und Prairie-indianer Nordamericas* [55] is the best general, comparative book for those who can read German.

For a very brief and convenient survey of Plains Indian culture, chapter 8, "The New Rich of the Plains: Early Residents of the Buffalo Country and Others Who Moved in with the Coming of the Horse," of *Red Man's America* [168], by Ruth Murray Underhill, is to be recommended. Symmes C. Oliver's *Ecology and Cultural Continuity as Contributing Factors in the Social Organization of the Plains Indians* [145] is also recommended for its compressed, scholarly overview of the interplay of different historical backgrounds and tribal social organization relative to special features of hunting, gathering, and gardening. Oliver's comparative tribal summaries are excellent, and the tables on pages 47 and 48 of his monograph are particularly helpful.

A succinct, comprehensive, and excellently illustrated summary of what is currently known about the prehistoric archeology of the Plains (12,000 B.C. to A.D. 1700) is given by Jesse D. Jennings in chapter 3 of his *Prehistory of North America* [71].

The Plains Area

The Great Plains form a geographic area defined by surface characteristics, climate, and vegetation. The pre-Europeans who inhabited the area are collectively called Plains Indians. This "collective" idea, however, was not held by the aboriginal inhabitants of the Plains. No Plains Indian is likely to have said of himself, "I am a Plains Indian," or of his people, "We are Plains Indians." Rather, his reference point was the band, or lineage, or tribal group — a very particularistic focus. Though he might wander afar, he did not experience "the Plains" as an identifiable entity and hence could not conceive of it as such. That remained for Euro-American explorer-naturalists of the nineteenth century, who could draw upon the comparative concepts of geography to classify physiographic zones and take note of their relations to indigenous life-ways.

The Great Plains also form a culture area: a geographic territory within which the human cultures tend to be distinctively similar in some significant aspects.

Although a number of traders, explorers, missionaries, and military men reported on various aspects of the Plains in their published journals, the first work to attempt to treat the Plains as an entity is Colonel Richard I. Dodge, *The Plains of the Great West and Their Inhabitants* [25], published in 1877. Part 1 provides a well-informed description of the variegated geology and climates of the Plains. Part 3, which is devoted to the tribes, is not generally reliable, nor does it attempt a comprehensive introduction to the Plains tribes at large. Walter P. Webb, *The Great Plains* [183], provides a modern synthesis of the geographic and human factors that combine to make the Plains a distinctive area, but it does not deal with Plains Indian ethnology.

Modern anthropological attempts to come to grips with the Great Plains as a physiographic and cultural concept emphasize just how much it is an idea, a mental construct, rather than an empirical entity in its own right. Clark Wissler, who first applied the notion of culture areas to the North American continent in his work *The American Indian* [201], included all of Utah and eastern Idaho, the western halves of Minnesota and Iowa, and virtually all of Missouri in his category of the Plains. He did, however, subdivide the vast Plains area into three distinguishable subclusters: the Central, Eastern Border, and Western Border. The cultures of the Central tribes were designated as typical for the Plains area. Subsistence was based on buffalo-hunting and limited gathering of roots and berries, without fishing or gardening. The skin tipi provided a portable dwelling. Transport included the dog (and later, horse) travois. No boats were manufactured or used. Clothing was made of dressed hides, and containers were fashioned from rawhide. Weaving was lacking, as were pottery and baskets. Social organization tended to be based on bands, or local groups, with use of the camp circle and of military societies for men. Ceremonially, the sun dance and sweat lodges were common. The Central tribes were identified as the Assiniboin, Arapaho, Blackfoot, Cheyenne, Comanche, Crow, Gros Ventre, Kiowa, Kiowa-Apache, Sarsi, and Teton Dakota.

Wissler's Eastern Border group had most of the traits of the nomadic Central tribes, with some added features. Subsistence was based on corn-growing and buffalo-hunting. Permanent villages were formed of earth lodges and tipis were used when out hunting. Pottery, basketry, and woven bags were in the household inventories, and simple skin boats were used to navigate the large rivers of the Missouri Valley. Maize ceremonies were more common than the sun dance. Wissler identified the Eastern Border tribes as the Arikara, Hidatsa, Iowa, Kansa, Mandan, Missouri, Omaha, Osage, Oto,

Pawnee, Ponca, Santee-Dakota, Yankton-Dakota, and the Wichita.

The Western Border cultures showed a subsistence base in which deer, antelope, and rabbits were more important than bison, while seed- and root-gathering were central to survival. Brush shelters were more common than the tipi, and basketry was highly developed. The Wind River Shoshone, Uintah, and Uncompahgre Ute are the only Western Border tribes Wissler mentions, although his area boundaries would embrace a number of Shoshonean groups in Utah and Idaho. Wissler identified thirty-one tribal groups as Plains Indians.

In contrast to Wissler, A. L. Kroeber, in his *Cultural and Natural Areas of Native North America* [81], was loath to accord the Plains any status as a culture area at all. "Essentially the view held," he wrote, "is that the Plains culture has been one of the well-developed and characterized cultures of North America only since the taking over of the horse from Europeans, and that previously there was no important Plains culture, the chief phases of the area being marginal to the richer cultures outside" (81, p. 76). In keeping with this view, Kroeber limited the Plains Indian culture area to the Southern Plains (occupied by the Comanche, Kiowa, and Kiowa-Apache in northwest Texas and western Oklahoma), and the Northern Plains (occupied by the Sarsi, Blackfoot, Atsina, Arapaho, Cheyenne, Crow, Teton Dakota, and Assiniboin, situated west of the hundredth meridian and east of the Rockies). Kroeber conceded only eleven tribes to be valid Plains Indians. Thus, he excluded all the horticultural village tribes of the Missouri Valley (the

Mandan, Hidatsa, Arikara, Pawnee, Dakota, etc.) as belonging to another and much more important culture area, the Prairie.

Waldo Wedel has recently synthesized the facts and implications of contemporary archeological research in the Plains and Prairie area in his *Prehistoric Man on the Great Plains* [185]. Nomadic hunting cultures utilizing dog transport are shown to have existed in the Plains as far back as ten to fifteen thousand years ago. Modern versions were still flourishing in the fifteenth and sixteenth centuries, before the introduction of the horse. The early settlements of village gardeners are now shown to date back to 700 B.C. Although clearly derived from the Mississippian archeological complex, they had definitely become native to the Plains. Hence, Wedel quite properly takes issue with Kroeber. He extends the eastern boundary of the Plains area to include the local cultures of the Missouri River system and its adjoining prairies. In chapter 2, Wedel presents the best summary of the physiography of the Plains and the distributions of vegetation and animal life that is readily available in the literature.

Wedel's archeologically based concept of the Plains culture area is essentially that of Wissler — without the eastward extension to the Mississippi River. Wedel's boundaries run along the eastern base of the Rocky Mountains, from southern Alberta to the Texas border of New Mexico; the eastern edges enclose the states of North and South Dakota, Nebraska, Kansas, Oklahoma, and the Texas panhandle.

Driver and Coffin's statistically based *Classification*

and Development of North American Indian Cultures [32] confirms the soundness of Wedel's determination of the Plains Indian culture area. Hence it is the one that has been adopted for use in this bibliography.

Prehistory

The earliest human inhabitants of the Plains arrived shortly before the end of the Ice Age in North America, possibly as early as 30,000 B.C. As evidenced by the skull found near Midland, Texas, in 1953, they were anatomically modern and are classified along with all contemporary human races as *Homo sapiens*. Fred Wendorf, Alex D. Krieger, Claude C. Albritton and T. Dale Stewart provide a comprehensive analysis of the Midland data from the points of view of archeology, geology, and physical anthropology in their valuable work *The Midland Discovery* [188].

The Paleo-Indians of the Plains, who are also identified as Big Game Hunters, flourished from about 12,000 B.C. to about 5,000 B.C. Waldo Wedel, in his *Prehistoric Man on the Great Plains* [185 chap. 3], ably summarizes all that is known of the first native Americans.

Between 5,000 B.C. and A.D. 500, climatic changes forced a change in the ways of life of the Paleo-Indians. With the extinction of Ice Age mammoths, camels, and bison, a gradual shift to seed- and root-gathering combined with incipient gardening was achieved. Settled villages with semisubterranean dwellings began to appear along the river courses of the eastern and central plains by A.D. 500. The next twelve hundred years constituted a period of continuous development of the horticultural, sedentary village complex, which finally reached its climax about A.D. 1700 in the cultures of the Mandan and Hidatsa Indians of North Dakota.

Hundreds of specialized archeological reports on the known sites of this later period of Plains prehistory have been published since the mid-1930s. Virtually all were stimulated by the revolutionary viewpoint advanced by William Duncan Strong, the father of modern Plains archeology, in his article "The Plains Culture Area in the Light of Archaeology" [164], which appeared in the *American Anthropologist* in 1933. Strong stressed the importance of the early appearance from the east of "at least semi-horticultural people in the central Plains," which had been previously unnoticed even though it "played at least an equal part with hunting in the economic life of the Central Plains." Strong's assessment introduced a new conception of the Plains in which the nomadic horse tribes, which had dominated ethnographic interest up to that time, were considered no more than a "thin and strikingly uniform veneer" that had spread over the central Plains in recent historical times. Strong issued a clarion call for immediate, intensive, coordinated work by historians, ethnologists, archeologists, geographers, and geologists to correct the balance. The result was the organization, in 1945, of the Inter-Agency Archeological Salvage Program of the United States Government, which combined the resources of the Smithsonian Institution, the National Park

Service, the Bureau of Reclamation, and the Corps of Engineers to assist various state and local agencies (mostly universities and historical societies) in systematic work associated with the great river dam and reclamation projects of the United States government. The organization and modes of operation of the whole gigantic enterprise are succinctly summarized by Don J. Lehmer in the opening chapters of his *Introduction to Middle Missouri Archeology* [90].

Excellent overall summaries of the prehistoric archeology of the sedentary horticultural cultures of the Plains from A.D. 500 to historical times are provided by Wedel, *Prehistoric Man on the Great Plains* [185], and Jennings, *Prehistory of North America* [71]. Wedel's work is the more detailed; Jennings's is more useful for a general overview. An equally valuable summation, although limited to the Middle Missouri River area, is Lehmer's *Introduction to Middle Missouri Archeology* [90]. For a very brief, but comprehensive and convenient, summation of the entire prehistory of the Plains, one should read Wedel's chapter "The Great Plains" [186] in Jesse D. Jennings and Edward Norbeck, *Prehistoric Man in the New World* [72].

Early Historic Contacts

In the spring of 1541 Coronado led his expedition eastward from the pueblos of New Mexico far out into the Central Plains. He visited encampments of nomadic, horseless, buffalo-hunting Indians (presumably Plains

Apaches), and in eastern Kansas-Nebraska he stopped
with sedentary gardeners who lived in large grass houses
— the Caddoans. George P. Hammond and Agapito Rey,
in *Narratives of the Coronado Expedition*, volume 2 [51],
provide a convenient English translation of these earliest
reports on Indians of the Plains, Herbert E. Bolton,
Spanish Exploration in the Southwest, 1542–1706 [9], offers
greater details from the observations of later Spanish
explorers in the area. Spanish relations with the Apaches
and hostile Comanches during the eighteenth century
are well summarized in Charles L. Kenner's *History of
New Mexican–Plains Indian Relations* [78]. The effect of
the Comanche adaptation of the horse to hit-and-run
attacks on the sedentary *rancherias* of the Plains-Apache
is analyzed by Frank R. Secoy in *Changing Military Patterns on the Great Plains* [157], and George E. Hyde covers
the same events in a highly readable and authentic man-
ner in the first five chapters of his *Indians of the High
Plains* [67]. Comanche-Texas hostilities are well chroni-
cled in Rupert N. Richardson's *The Comanche Barrier to
South Plains Settlement* [151].

For historical contacts in the northwestern Plains
area, beginning around A.D. 1700, the most informative
original journals are Charles N. Bell, ed., *The Journal of
Henry Kelsey (1691–1692: The First White Man to Reach the
Saskatchewan from Hudson Bay* [4]; Anthony Hendry, *York
Factory to the Blackfeet Country: The Journal of Anthony
Hendry, 1754–55* [57]; and Alexander Henry and David
Thompson, *New Light on the Early History of the Greater*

Northwest, 1799–1814 [58]. For the Middle Missouri River sedentary, gardening tribes the *Journals and Letters of Pierre Gaultier de Varennes de la Vérendrye and His Sons*, edited by Lawrence J. Burpee [89], are of great value and interest in view of the fact that horses had not yet reached the Mandans when the La Vérendryes first visited them in 1738.

Original sources on the Plains Indians in the first half of the nineteenth century are the journals of traders, explorers, soldiers, missionaries, and artists. Of these, Reuben Gold Thwaites's eight-volume edition of Meriwether Lewis, *The Original Journals of the Lewis and Clark Expedition, 1804–1806* [94] stands without peer, but for the nonspecialist James K. Hosmer's two-volume reprint of Lewis's excellent *History of the Expedition of Captains Lewis and Clark, 1804–5–6* [93], originally published in 1814, has all the necessary detail. The expedition wintered among the Mandans, and the report has much of interest to offer on the Missouri River tribes and their relations to their nomadic neighbors.

George Catlin's numerous paintings and journal observations on tribes of the upper Plains area can be studied in several forms. A high-quality paperback reprint, including more than three hundred paintings, of Catlin's *Letters and Notes on the Manners, Customs, and Conditions of North American Indians* [17] is now readily available.

Travels in the Interior of North America [132], the observations of Prince Maximilian of Wied-Neuwied, who visited the Mandan and Hidatsa in 1833, provides another generally reliable early view of several important tribes.

Excellent papers on the Sioux, Arikaras, Assiniboines, Crees, and Crows written by Edwin Thompson Denig, who served as agent for the American Fur Company on the upper Missouri from 1833 to 1856, are collected in his *Five Indian Tribes of the Upper Missouri* [22].

The fur trade, plus the introduction of the horse and the gun, had a catalytic effect upon the lives and cultures of the tribes of the Plains. A concise general summary of the trade is provided in John C. Ewers, *Indian Life on the Upper Missouri* [38], while specific analysis of its effects, buttressed by careful historical scholarship, may be found in Oscar Lewis, *The Effects of White Contact upon Blackfoot Culture* [95]; Joseph Jablow, *The Cheyenne in Plains Indian Trade Relations, 1795–1840* [69]; and Frank R. Secoy, *Changing Military Patterns on the Great Plains* [157]. Preston Holder has written a good summary, intended for the lay reader, of the general effects of white contact and trade upon the historical development of Plains Indian tribes in their relations to each other and the incursive Europeans. It is in paperback and titled *The Hoe and the Horse on the Plains* [62].

The spread of the European horse and its adaptation to Indian life on the Plains has received a good deal of attention from anthropologists. The early view, set forth by Clark Wissler in his article "The Influence of the Horse in the Development of Plains Culture" [200], held that among the nomadic tribes the whole basic structure of the later Indian horse culture was in existence before the introduction of the horse. Horses merely intensified existing culture patterns.

The modern view recognizes the pre-European existence of nomadic hunting cultures with dog-traction on the Plains but accepts William Duncan Strong's [164] proposition that the nineteenth-century horse cultures were indeed a transformation of far-reaching significance. The manifestations of Plains Indian horse culture in all its rich detail are best set forth in John C. Ewers's *The Horse in Blackfoot Indian Culture* [36]. This work also sums up what is currently known about the history of the spread of the horse from New Mexico and Texas via the Comanche-Shoshone and the Kiowa to the more northern tribes.

Tribal Cultures

Village Tribes of the Missouri Basin

As indicated in the discussion of Plains prehistoric archeology and historical contacts, the sedentary gardening tribes of the Missouri River basin were flourishing long before the arrival of the Europeans and Americans. Although welcomed for the goods and temporary prosperity they brought, the early traders inadvertently introduced measles and smallpox, to which the Indians had no immunity. The whites fought no wars with the Mandan and Hidatsa, but severe epidemics in 1780–82, and again in 1837, decimated the tribes and forced a consolidation of their villages. The nine villages the Mandan had in 1750 were reduced to two by 1776. The

Hidatsa suffered equally severely. What disease failed to do, Sioux marauders from the south and east completed in the last decades of the eighteenth century and the first third of the nineteenth. The Arikara, although they waged a minor war with the Americans under Leavenworth in the 1820s, were likewise nearly destroyed by disease and the Sioux. The handful of survivors of the three once-great village peoples came together under United States protection on the Fort Berthold Reservation in 1845 and after.

By the time the village tribes began to receive ethnographic attention, which was not until the early part of the twentieth century, most of their old way of life was long gone. As a result, it has been possible for anthropologists to add only a little to what early observers had previously recorded. This accounts for the relative brevity of the bibliographical sections on the village tribes, compared with the much fuller sections on the nomadic horse tribes that follow later.

Mandan

The matrilineal Mandans may well be dubbed "The Parisians of the Plains," for it was among these people that the long development of the prehistoric agricultural buffalo-hunting complex of the sedentary villages reached its richest climax. With the Hidatsa, their villages formed trading centers in both prehistoric and historical times to which lesser tribes were drawn. The basic general book on the Mandan is the Peabody Museum monograph by George F. Will and Herbert J. Spinden, *The*

Mandans: A Study of Their Culture, Archaeology and Language [192]. Much more thorough and detailed, but hard to comprehend because of its diffuse form of organization and writing is Alfred W. Bowers's *Mandan Social and Ceremonial Organization* [11]. In 1967, a centennial edition of the artist George Catlin's eyewitness account of the Mandan's great religious ceremony, the Okipa, as performed in 1833, was published by Yale University Press. This volume, *O-Kee-Pa* [16], contains thirteen colored reproductions of Catlin's original Okipa paintings and is a must for anyone interested in the Missouri River Indians. Letters 10–22 in Catlin's *Letters and Notes* [17] are devoted to his observations of the Mandan. Finally, a very well organized account of Mandan culture history from prehistoric times through the near extinction of the tribe by smallpox and Sioux assaults in the first half of the nineteenth century is the article by Edward M. Bruner [14] in Edward H. Spicer, *Perspectives in American Indian Culture Change*. Recent archeological materials on the Mandan are ably, though technically summarized by W. Raymond Wood in his River Basin Surveys monograph *An Interpretation of Mandan Culture History* [204].

Hidatsa (also called Minnetaree)

These near neighbors of the Mandans are well covered in four classic monographs. First, there is Washington Matthews's early study, published in 1877 as *Ethnography and Philology of the Hidatsa Indians* [131]. Gilbert L. Wilson provides an indispensable descriptive analysis of gardening practices in *Agriculture of the Hidatsa Indians* [193]. A more generalized introductory treatment of Plains village agriculture may be found in George F. Will and George W. Hyde, *Corn among the Indians of the Upper Missouri* [191]. *The Horse and Dog in Hidatsa Culture* [194], also by Gilbert L. Wilson, provides data on another facet of Hidatsa economic life. However, for an overview of the Hidatsa in one volume, the most satisfactory work is Alfred W. Bowers's *Hidatsa Social and Ceremonial Organization* [12]. Martha Warren Beckwith's comparative study *Mandan-Hidatsa Myths and Ceremonies* [3] is a very worthwhile supplementary source.

Arikara

The Arikaras are a Pawnee offshoot who moved northward into close proximity to the Mandans during the eighteenth century. No really systematic account of the Arikaras has as yet been published. The best available general materials may be found in Annie H. Abel's edition of Pierre Antoine Tabeau, *Tabeau's Narrative of Loisel's Expedition to the Upper Missouri* [166]; Edwin Denig, *Five Indian Tribes of the Upper Missouri* [22]; Charles E. De Land,, *The Aborigines of South Dakota* [19]; and Ernest S. Macgowan, "The Arikara Indians" [120]. A complete bibliography covering a number of specialized articles devoted to fragments of Arikara culture may be found in George P. Murdock and Timothy J. O'Leary, *Ethnographic Bibliography of North America* [140], volume 5, pages 36–41.

Omaha

The patrilineal Omaha form an interesting comparison to the Mandan. Early in this century Francis La Flesche, himself an Omaha, and Alice C. Fletcher published their famous work *The Omaha Tribe* [40], a totally comprehensive ethnography. In the 1930s, Reo F. Fortune and Margaret Mead carried out joint fieldwork among the Omaha that resulted in a functional study by Fortune called *Omaha Secret Societies* [41] and an account of social change in Omaha life by Mead, who gave the tribe the pseudonym "Antlers" in her brief volume *The Changing Culture of an Indian Tribe* [134]. A useful historical summary of the Omaha tribe is provided by G. Hubert Smith in a volume that also contains the official findings of the Indian Claims Commission with respect to the Omaha tribal land land claims against the government of the United States [173].

Osage

The fascinating history of the Osage tribe, near relatives of the Omahas, Poncas, Kansas, and Quapaws, is succinctly summed up in a highly readable little book *The Osage People* [1], written by W. David Baird, a historian, for the Indian Tribal Series. John Joseph Mathews has written two much more extensive histories of the Osages. *The Osages: Children of the Middle Waters* [130] is a fine narrative history of the tribe from pre-Columbian times into the twentieth century. *Wah'kon-tah: The Osage and the White Man's Road* [129] is a perceptive account of the reservation life and attitudes of the Osages seen through the person of Major Laban J. Miles, Indian agent to the Osages in the 1870s and 1880s. But for the student who wishes to steep himself in the mystic thought and ritual expression of the Osage world view there are incomparable recordings of tribal rites prepared by Francis La Flesche and published in five parts by the Bureau of American Ethnology under the titles *The Osage Tribe: Rites of the Chiefs; Sayings of the Ancient Men* [83]; *The Osage Tribe: The Rite of Vigil* [84], *The Osage Tribe: Two Versions of the Child-naming Rite* [85]; *The Osage Tribe: Rite of the WA-XÓ-BE* [86]; and *War Ceremony and Peace Ceremony of the Osage Indians* [87]. In addition, the very serious student of Osage history is now well served by the five volumes of reports on Osage ethnohistory prepared and submitted in evidence for consideration by the Indian Claims Commission, plus the findings of fact and opinions by the commission itself [174]. The research papers include a comprehensive introductory summary of research on the Osage, written by Fred W. Voget, and Alice Marriott adds a complete bibliography of all relevant basic research references on the Osage and their history. The Osage archeological background is exhaustively covered by Carl H. Chapman. The social and political achievements and vicissitudes of the Osage Nation are covered by Dale R. Henning for the period 1775–1818.

Ponca

The Ponca, according to tradition, split from the Omaha perhaps three hundred years ago and became the northernmost of the Degiha-speaking Sioux. Their habitat lay along both sides of the Niobrara River, above and below its juncture with the Missouri in northeastern Nebraska. Very little is known about this small village tribe. What is known is economically summarized in James H. Howard's recent monograph *The Ponca Tribe* [63], and also in Joseph Jablow's study for the Indian Claims Commission, *Ethnology of the Ponca* [177].

Iowa and Oto

These two Siouxan tribes lived along the Missouri River just above and below the confluence of the Platte, in eastern Nebraska. Alanson B. Skinner's *Ethnology of the Ioway Indians* [159] covers virtually all of consequence that has been written on this little-known tribe. Even less has been written on the Oto, close kinsmen to the Iowa; for a general summary of the tribe and its culture one should refer to William Whitman's monograph, *The Oto* [190]. Archeological and historical data with respect to the exact location of the Oto may be found in the Indian Claims Commission volume, *Oto and Missouri Indians* [175].

Pawnee

Of the Caddoan-speaking tribes of the southeastern portion of the Plains, the Pawnees are the most studied and the best known. A remarkable people who lived in earth lodges, gardened, and hunted, they are notable for their elaborate ceremonialism and prowess in war. They had, however, a singular proclivity for making enemies of all neighboring tribes and failing to cooperate among their several bands, and a stubborn incapacity to form alliances necessary to military survival. Decimated by the Sioux and by smallpox, and culturally assassinated by United States government intent and mismanagement (ironically most severely by the Quaker administration of the Indian service in the 1870s) they have a peculiarly tragic history.

As an introduction to the Pawnees, the best starting point is the compact historical summary and general ethnographic sketch offered by Wendell H. Oswalt in chapter 6 of his book for the layman, *This Land Was Theirs* [146]. Next there is *Pawnee Indian Societies* by James R. Murie [141], himself a Pawnee. It is a basic monograph, readable and informative on the nature of Pawnee sacred and secular societies; it also includes additional ethnographic data of importance. More extensive information on the social organization of the northern, or Skidi, division of the Pawnees is provided in George A. Dorsey and James R. Murie's monograph *Notes on Skidi Pawnee Society* [31]. Additional ethnological and historical information prepared by John L. Champe, Franklin Fenenga, Thomas M. Griffiths, and Waldo R. Wedel for the information of the Indian Claims Commission may be found in the American Indian Ethnohistory volume *Pawnee and Kansa (Kaw) Indians* [176]. An exceedingly detailed account of the Pawnee life-style and world view has been drawn together by the contemporary anthropologist Gene Weltfish in *The Lost Universe*

[187], a sophisticated anthropological record and interpretation of a culture that is no more.

Waldo R. Wedel's *Introduction to Pawnee Archeology*
[184] details the archeological discoveries relating to
Pawnee prehistory and includes a praiseworthy synthesis
of historical and ethnographic facts. Also to be com-
mended as a more general historical coverage of the
Pawnees is *Pawnee Indians*, by the indefatigable and interesting chronicler of western tribes George E. Hyde
[65]. Hyde's account, which carries Pawnee history up to
1890, is appropriately supplemented by Alexander
Lesser's skilled analysis of the disintegration of Pawnee
culture and the reasons for it in his monograph *The
Pawnee Ghost Dance Hand Game* [92]. Lesser focuses upon
the temporary renaissance of Pawnee culture in response
to the ghost dance movement of the 1890s.

The rich and colorful Pawnee mythology has been
comprehensively recorded in two solid studies by George
A. Dorsey: *The Pawnee: Mythology* [29], and *Traditions of
the Skidi Pawnee* [27]. George Bird Grinnell's *Pawnee Hero
Stories and Folk-tales* [44] is a collection of Pawnee legends
and war stories, as opposed to ceremonial myths.

The Nomadic Tribes

The nomadic tribes of the Plains, as they existed
between A.D. 1750 and 1875, may be conveniently placed
in two groups. First, there are the people who were
originally gardeners in the woodlands and prairies lying
east of the Plains and who gave up sedentary farming for

nomadic hunting. This group consists of the Algonkian-speaking Arapahos, Gros Ventres, and Cheyennes, as well as the Siouxan-speaking Crows. All were located in the north central and northwest portions of the Plains and were strongly influenced by the cultures of the sedentary village tribes in prehistoric and protohistoric times.

Second, there are those tribes who apparently have been nomadic hunters from time immemorial. All occupied peripheral positions in the Plains area, and most were very recent immigrants from outside the Plains. The Kiowas are the sole exception, for they appear to have occupied their territory since late prehistoric times. Other tribes in the group include the Kiowa-Apaches and the Comanches in the south; the Blackfeet in the northwest; and the Assiniboines and Plains Crees in the northeast.

Arapaho

Alfred L. Kroeber's fundamental monograph *The Arapaho* [79] is the comprehensive anthropological account of Arapaho life and culture. Henry Elkin, however, gives a good compact summary and traces the changes and adaptation in Arapaho culture through the reservation period down to the mid-1930s in a lengthy chapter, "The Northern Arapaho of Wyoming" [34] in *Acculturation in Seven American Indian Tribes*, edited by Ralph Linton [99]. Another good introductory source, intended for the layman, is *The Arapahoes*, by Virginia C.

Trenholm [167]. Several special studies provide great detail on particular aspects of Arapaho culture and history. Notable among these are George A. Dorsey, *The Arapaho Sun Dance* [26], Frances Densmore, *Cheyenne and Arapaho Music* [24], George A. Dorsey and Alfred L. Kroeber on *Traditions of the Arapaho* [30], a rich record of the oral literature (folklore and mythology) of the tribe, and Fred Eggan, "The Cheyenne and Arapaho Kinship System" [33]. The United States Indian Claims Commission volume *Arapaho-Cheyenne Indians* [169] includes several historical and ethnological essays on the movements and modern economic conditions of the Southern Cheyennes and the Arapahoes, along with the commission's own statement of findings of fact and of opinions. Growing up among the Arapahoes is well described in *Arapaho Child Life and Its Cultural Background*, by Sister Inez Hilger [59], and in an interesting biography of an Arapaho boyhood, *The Arapaho Way*, recorded by Althea Bass [2].

Cheyenne

The Cheyennes are one of the best documented and most thoroughly studied of the nomadic Plains tribes. The known historical and archeological facts of their movement from the woodlands of Minnesota across the Missouri out onto the western high plains are objectively given and evaluated by W. Raymond Wood in his archeological report on a protohistoric sedentary village site in South Dakota, *Biesterfeldt* [205], pages 57–76. The basic

resource on the Cheyennes is George Bird Grinnell's
two-volume classic, *The Cheyenne Indians* [48]. For a relatively brief modern anthropological description and
interpretation of Cheyenne culture as it existed about
1860, there is E. Adamson Hoebel's culture case study
The Cheyennes [61].

From the 1850s and continuing for a quarter of a
century, relations between the Cheyennes and the
United States government were marked by numerous
disputes and wars. The western historian Donald J.
Berthrong has written a reliable account, largely from
government records, of the conflicts between the United
States and the Southern Cheyenne in his *The Southern
Cheyennes* [5]. From the Indian viewpoint, a Northern
Cheyenne historian, John Stands in Timber, with Margot Liberty as his amanuensis, has recorded in *Cheyenne
Memories* [163] the famous Cheyenne wars of the last
century as well as numerous aspects of the old way of life
and early days on the reservation. The really definitive
work on the Cheyenne wars, however, is Grinnell's fascinating book *The Fighting Cheyennes* [46]. It covers all
major Cheyenne battles from 1820 to the slaughter of the
Cheyennes in the Fort Robinson Outbreak in 1879 and
does so in the words of the Cheyennes themselves. *By
Cheyenne Campfires* [49], also by Grinnell, is a popular
collection of Cheyenne myths, legends, and war stories;
Grinnell's *When Buffalo Ran* [47] is a delightful biography
about a Cheyenne's youth.

An even more fascinating account is the highly personal and sensitive autobiography of the Cheyenne

leader Wooden Leg, recorded and written by Thomas B. Marquis [125].

The ceremonies of the Cheyenne have been described by Grinnell [48, volume 2], but in addition, the sun dance was thoroughly recorded by George A. Dorsey [28]; its performance in the mid-twentieth century is sympathetically and richly described by Father Peter J. Powell, whose *Sweet Medicine* [149] is a major contribution.

Another volume, which contains much detailed information about Cheyenne interpersonal relations in the form of verbatim accounts of Cheyenne legal disputes within the tribe, is *The Cheyenne Way* by Karl N. Llewellyn and E. Adamson Hoebel [100]. In addition to its lively cases of Cheyenne law and government in action, this book includes important materials on the method and theory of studying unwritten tribal law systems.

Gros Ventre (Atsina)

The literature on this Algonkian tribe is essentially limited to the works of Kroeber, Cooper, and Flannery, but what it lacks in numbers is amply compensated for by the quality and comprehensiveness of the contributions of these three anthropologists. Kroeber did his field studies among the Gros Ventre early in this century and published a somewhat cursory summary of the tribal culture in 1907: *The Ethnology of the Gros Ventre* [80]. Fortunately, Father John M. Cooper turned his attention to the Gros Ventre with three successive field trips in

1938–40, which resulted in one of the best in-depth accounts of any Plains Indian religion: *The Gros Ventres of Montana. Part II. Religion and Ritual* [18]. Flannery, a younger associate of Father Cooper's, followed up his fieldwork with field investigations of her own, combining the results in an excellent historical and descriptive account of tribal organization in her *The Gros Ventres of Montana. Part I. Social Life* [39].

Crow

The Siouxan-speaking Crows are an offshoot of the Missouri River Hidatsa. In their westward migrations to the foot of the Rocky Mountains, the Crows became buffalo-hunters and nomadic warriors on the Montana and Wyoming Plains. The literature on the Crows is rich and varied, ranging from the vivid firsthand accounts of the nineteenth century "squaw-men" Beckwourth and LeForge, through the Crow biographies recorded by Frank Linderman, to the meticulous ethnographic studies done early in the present century by Robert H. Lowie.

Among Lowie's many publications on the Crows is a fine general book, *The Crow Indians* [109]. This provides the only comprehensive introduction to all aspects of tribal life and beliefs. In addition, for the reader who seeks detailed information on more specialized aspects of Crow Indian culture there are the following American Museum of Natural History monographs, all written by Lowie before 1924: *Crow Indian Art* [107]; *The Material*

Culture of the Crow Indians [108]; *Military Societies of the Crow Indians* [103]; *Myths and Traditions of the Crow Indians* [105]; *Social Life of the Crow Indians* [102]; *The Sun Dance of the Crow Indians* [104]; and *The Tobacco Society of the Crow Indians* [106]. An additional work by Lowie is *The Crow Language* [110], published in 1941.

A brief layman's introduction to the Crows, their culture and history, interesting but not profound, is the Indian Tribal Series volume by Dale K. McGinnis and Floyd W. Sharrock, *The Crow People* [119]. A more comprehensive introduction, but not as authoritative as Lowie's [109], is the summary *Crow Indians*, prepared for the Indian Claims Commission hearings by Norman B. Plummer [171].

The books of the three Americans who lived for many years among the Crows with their Crow Indian wives are fascinating reading and provide much firsthand information on Crow daily life. James Beckwourth, a mulatto, was a mountain man who settled in with the Crows in the 1820s and 1830s. In the view of Lowie, Beckwourth was a Munchausen in the recital of his own deeds, admirably correct in his account of the martial life of the Crows, and weak in his understanding of Crow Indian religion. Beckwourth's memoirs were edited and published by Thomas D. Bonner [10]. Zenas Leonard [91] wrote eyewitness accounts of war and burial customs, hunting, and other aspects of daily routine in the Crow camps in the first half of the 1830s. Thomas H. LeForge married into the Crow tribe and lived as a white man among the Crow during the last half of the nineteenth century. His useful memoirs have been edited by Thomas B. Marquis as *Memoirs of a White Crow Indian* [124].

Finally, thanks to the sympathetic assistance of Frank Linderman, old frontiersman and author on the Crow, Cheyenne, and Sioux, we have the autobiographies of a Crow chief, *Plenty-coups* [96], and a Crow Indian medicine woman, *Pretty-shield* [97], while yet another, *Two Leggings* [142], has been recently written by Peter Nabokov.

Teton Dakota (Lakota Sioux)

The Tetons, who lived on the open prairies between the Upper Mississippi and the Missouri Rivers before A.D. 1660, differed from Yanktonai Sioux, who occupied the woodlands of southeastern Minnesota and northeastern Iowa, and the Santee Sioux, who lived for the most part east of the Mississippi. The latter were hunter/gatherers (especially of wild rice) and incipient gardeners. The Tetons relied on neither wild rice nor gardening, except in very small degree. They were nomadic buffalo-hunters well before they moved out onto the Plains. Radisson, who in 1680 was the first white to visit Minnesota, called them "The Nation of the Beefe." Like their early neighbors the Cheyennes, the Tetons evidently began to feel tribal pressures from the east even before the arrival of European traders and missionaries. Shortly after 1660, the Tetons began a southwestward migration to the headwaters of the Minnesota River and the Red

River of the North. Continuing in the same direction, they reached the Missouri in South Dakota in the early 1700s and ejected the Arikara from their traditional villages, completing their crossing of the Missouri about A.D. 1785. By A.D. 1825 they had engulfed all of South Dakota (leaving the James River valley in the east to the Yanktonai, who followed them), establishing the Oglala division in a wide area surrounding the Black Hills (including parts of Wyoming and Nebraska) with the Hunkpapa, Blackfoot, and Sans-arc divisions immediately to the north of them, while the Minneconjou division lingered just west of the Missouri below the North Dakota border.

An excellent short account of Teton Sioux migrations and historic contacts with the fur trade and United States government is presented in Scudder Mekeel's "A Short History of the Teton Dakota" [135]. A briefer summary of the same topic is available in James A. Hanson's interesting volume *Metal Weapons, Tools, and Ornaments of the Teton Dakota Indians* [53], pages 1–10. A fuller treatment may be found in Doane Robinson's extensive monograph *A History of the Dakota or Sioux Indians* [152], or, if a less weighty and more popularized treatment of Oglala Sioux history is preferred, *Red Cloud's Folk*, by George E. Hyde [64], serves very well. His volume on the Brulé division of the Tetons, *Spotted Tail's Folk* [68], is even better. Wesley R. Hurt, in his *Dakota Sioux Indians* [178, vol. II], offers a clear and comprehensive summary statement on the tribe. The Indian Claims Commission's [178, vol. IV] evaluation of the Sioux Indian land claims and the validity of the ethnohistorical evidence bearing on them holds great contemporary interest and importance.

A lively firsthand description of Sioux activity at the height of their power in the northern plains during the period 1833–56, is given by the American fur trader Edwin Thompson Denig in his *Five Indian Tribes of the upper Missouri*, edited by John C. Ewers [22].

Strangely enough, perhaps because of the dispersed nature of the Teton Sioux tribal divisions by the middle of the nineteenth century, a few comprehensive studies of their culture as a total social system have been written. Royal B. Hassrick is one author who has undertaken the challenge in his book *The Sioux* [56]. His work is well balanced and objective, although some readers may be shocked to read his characterization of the Sioux as vainglorious, a people who "could hardly help being aware of their power. [They] were far more than aware: they were overbearing in their vanity" (p. 67). Sonia Bleeker has also written a work called *The Sioux Indians* [7], and Mari Sandoz's *These Were the Sioux* [154], is, like all her works, a fine piece of authorship. Shorter introductions to Teton Sioux culture may be found in O. Eldon Johnson's section "The Teton Dakota," pp. 350–81 in his chapter on the tribes of the Great Plains [73] in Robert F. Spencer and Jesse D. Jennings, et al., *The Native Americans* [160], and in Jeanette Mirsky, "The Dakota" [136]. *The Sioux People*, by Joseph H. Cash [15], is a short, popular introduction.

While it has been difficult for anthropologists or

other writers to undertake the task of synthesizing Sioux culture as a whole, no tribe is as well represented by personal expressions of their tribal life as are the Tetons. Luther Standing Bear heads the tribal authors with his *Land of the Spotted Eagle* [162] and *My People the Sioux* [161]. *Black Elk Speaks* [143], written down by John G. Neihardt, is a somewhat embroidered but interesting expression of one Sioux's view of the old life. And again, Black Elk eloquently protrays the substance and meaning of a major Sioux ritual complex in his *The Sacred Pipe* [13], edited by Joseph Epes Brown.

Special aspects of Teton culture have received detailed study by a number of ethnologists. The following may be listed as most valuable and of general interest: on music, Harry W. Paige, *Songs of the Teton Sioux* [147], and Frances Dinsmore's classic *Teton Sioux Music* [23]; on crafts, Clark Wissler, "Decorative Art of the Sioux Indians" [195], Carrie A. Lyford, *Quill and Beadwork of the Western Sioux* [112], and James A. Hanson on metal artifacts and ornaments [53].

The traditional sun dance of the Oglala is thoroughly described by J. R. Walker in *The Sun Dance and Other Ceremonies of the Ogalala Division of the Teton Dakota* [181] and by the Dakota anthropologist Ella Deloria in "The Sun Dance of the Oglala Sioux" [20]. The warrior and ceremonial societies of the Oglala are also reliably recorded by Wissler in another American Museum of Natural History monograph [198].

The Sioux were leaders in the ill-fated Ghost Dance movement of the 1890s, a messianic movement that promised the return of the beloved dead and of the myriad of buffalo that once roamed their country, and the elysian revival of their lost way of life, along with a cataclysmic elimination of the whites. James A. Mooney's classic study *The Ghost Dance Religion* [138] has stood for decades as the definitive descriptive analysis of the events and causes of the movement. However, Robert M. Utley's *Last Days of the Sioux Nation* [179] has added new materials and a more objective, modern interpretation. The Plains Indian Ghost Dance is also treated in its broader human psychological setting in a book of magnificent scholarship and readability by Weston La Barre, *The Ghost Dance* [82].

The mid-twentieth-century events at Wounded Knee are still too recent to have produced reliable accounts. However, several good researches on the lives and character of the contemporary descendants of the old warriors are available. Foremost is *Warriors without Weapons* [121], by Gordon Macgregor, a skilled anthropologist and one-time superintendent of the Office of Indian Affairs Pine Ridge Agency. Vine Deloria's polemic in *Custer Died for Your Sins* [21] not withstanding, Macgregor's book is a good account. The distinguished psychoanalyst Erik Erikson has written penetratingly on contemporary Sioux child training and education in his *Childhood and Society* [35]. George E. Hyde in *A Sioux Chronicle* [66] covers the period 1879–90, after the Sioux were confined to reservation life.

Blackfoot (also Blackfeet, including the Piegan)

The Blackfoot are the earliest Algonkian-speaking Indians to reach the Plains. There are no records or native traditions of their migration from the eastern woodlands, where presumably they must have lived. They were well-established buffalo-hunters and gatherers, without horses, located in the northwest margins of the Plains in Saskatchewan and Alberta, remote from the British trading factories on Hudson Bay and from the Spaniards to the south. Horses and a few guns reached them via other Indian tribes before they were visited by Fench traders for the first time in the 1730s, but the Hudson's Bay Company made no attempt to contact them until 1754. Subsequently, although devastated by smallpox in 1781, they prospered in trade and well-being through the nineteenth century.

John C. Ewers is the leading contemporary student of the Blackfeet; his book *The Blackfeet* [37], written for laymen, is the best general introduction to the tribe. Ewers's "Ethnological Report on the Blackfeet and Gros Ventre Tribes" [170] is another authoritative introduction. However, Ewers's specialized study *The Horse in Blackfoot Indian Culture* [36] is a much more intensively researched report, a model for all future studies on adoption of the new mode of transport by Plains Indians. Oscar Lewis, in his first published work, *The Effects of White Contact upon Blackfoot Culture* [95], convincingly showed how the fur trade led to far-reaching transformations not only in material culture but also in marriage, social organization, and native religion.

Blackfoot culture as it existed in the nineteenth century is given detailed attention in a number of its aspects in several books and monographs. Basic are Clark Wissler's *Material Culture of the Blackfoot Indians* [196]; *Societies and Dance Associations of the Blackfoot Indians* [199]; *Ceremonial Bundles of the Blackfoot Indians* [197]; and *The Sun Dance of the Blackfoot Indians* [202]. Life among the Blackfoot as experienced by a white man in the last century is recorded in James W. Schultz's *Blackfeet and Buffalo* [156]. Blackfoot folklore and mythology have been recorded and published by George Bird Grinnell in his *Blackfoot Lodge Tales* [45], by James W. Schultz, *Blackfeet Tales* [155], and by Clark Wissler and D. C. Duvall, *Mythology of the Blackfoot Indians* [203].The Grinnell and Schultz volumes are written for lay readers. The Wissler and Duvall monograph is primarily for professional folklorists.

The Blackfeet of modern times are the subject of three useful books: *Tribe under Trust*, by Lucien M. Hanks and Jane Richardson Hanks [52]; *Modern Blackfeet*, by Malcolm McFee [117]; and *Changing Configurations in the Social Organization of a Blackfoot Tribe during the Reserve Period*, by Esther S. Goldfrank [43].

Assiniboine

The Assiniboines are yet another Siouxan tribe that was once located in Minnesota and then made the westward migration. As Yanktonai Dakota, they were not part of the direct westward movement of the Tetons, but migrated northward to the country between Lake Superior and Hudson Bay about A.D. 1600 to 1640, then westward toward Lake Athabaska (A.D. 1650–1700), and finally southward into the northernmost reaches of the

Plains lying above the Missouri River after 1750. It was they who escorted Larpenteur to his first meeting with Mandans.

Relatively little has been published on the Assiniboines. Robert H. Lowie did anthropological fieldwork among them early in this century and published the only general ethnological account of the tribe, *The Assiniboine* [101]. David Rodnick's *The Fort Belknap Assiniboine of Montana* [153] covers the Assiniboine now located on the United States side of the border, and Diamond Jenness has written a succinct introductory overview of the historical movements of the tribe, and its mode of livelihood and culture, in chapter 20 of his *Indians of Canada* [70]. An Assiniboine view of themselves is told in simple language by James Larpenteur Long, edited by Michael S. Kennedy, in *The Assiniboines* [77].

Three convenient early historical sources on the Assiniboines as seen by trappers who had close contact with them are the memoirs of Pierre G. V. La Vérendrye, *Journals and Letters* [89], Charles Larpenteur, *Forty Years a Fur Trader on the Upper Missouri* [88], and for the nineteenth century, Edwin Thompson Denig, *Five Indian Tribes of the Upper Missouri* [22].

For supplemental readings, the biography *Tatanga Mani*, by John MacEwan [116], and the autobiography *Recollections of an Assiniboine Chief*, by Dan Kennedy [76], are generally worthwhile.

Plains Cree

Allies and near neighbors of the Assiniboine, the

Plains Cree were the very last of the eastern Woodland tribes to migrate into the Plains. The movement took place wholly after the establishment of Hudson's Bay Company posts, from which the Cree obtained guns and hence pressed southwest into Saskatchewan and northern Montana. Very quickly, some bands became wholly horse-mounted buffalo-hunters and typical warrior-raiders of the Plains with military societies and the sun dance.

Only one comprehensive study of the Plains Cree was ever made, that by David G. Mandelbaum, *The Plains Cree* [123], A sketchy, earlier piece by Alanson B. Skinner, *Political Organization, Cults and Ceremonies of the Plains–Ojibway and Plains–Cree Indians* [158] can be used as a supplement to Mandelbaum, and readers interested in mythology and the Algonkian language will find Leonard Bloomfield's *Plains Cree Texts* [8] a treasure trove.

Kiowa

The Kiowas are especially interesting as a Plains Indian group, for though little is known of their early history, they are known to have established themselves in the southern plains before European influences began to make themselves felt among the western tribes. Unlike most of the nomadic buffalo-hunters, the Kiowas were not recent immigrants from areas peripheral to the Plains, although their traditions place their origins in the mountains of Montana.

Mildred P. Mayhall's *The Kiowas* [133], provides a

general summary of the tribe, written primarily for the lay reader. For the "feel" of Kiowa life, *The Ten Grandmothers* [126], by Alice L. Marriott, is a superb piece of writing—fictional, to be sure, but expressing a true and intimate understanding of Kiowa history and culture for the period beginning in 1847 and continuing up to World War II.

The classical account of the Kiowas is, of course, James Mooney's *Calendar History of the Kiowa Indians* [139]. Essentially, it is an interpretive presentation of the annual historical events by which several Kiowas pictorially identified each year from 1832 to 1892 by mnemonic devices painted on hides. Marriott has also covered the effect of white contact upon the Kiowas in a resource book written for use in secondary school social studies courses, entitled *Kiowa Years* [128].

Very little has been written on the Kiowa from the ethnological point of view. Three brief special-topic monographs do stand out, however. *Rank and Warfare among the Plains Indians* [137], by Bernard Mishkin, is a study of class ranking among Kiowa males. The second, by Jane Richardson, *Law and Status among the Kiowa Indians* [150], is a dynamic case study of Kiowa internal disputes and the ways they were legally settled. Kiowas' use of their plant environment is carefully recorded in Paul A. Vestal and Richard E. Schultes, *The Economic Botany of the Kiowa Indians* [180].

No written ethnological or historical reports on the Kiowa and Comanche tribes were prepared for the Indian Claims Commission hearings on these two tribes, but the two volumes of testimony of anthropologists and Indians, [172], which was presented orally or in sign language, are certainly of great interest.

Kiowa folklore has been well recorded. Elsie Clews Parsons's *Kiowa Tales* [148] provides the conventional folklorist's coverage. Alice L. Marriott, in *Saynday's People* [127], includes both Kiowa life and stories presented in a more narrative style, while Col. Wilbur S. Nye, former U.S. Army historian at Ft. Sill, Oklahoma, presents Kiowa tales in an even more popularized vein in *Bad Medicine and Good* [144]. An extensive Kiowa vocabulary by John P. Harrington may be found in Bulletin 84 of the Bureau of American Ethnology [54].

Kiowa-Apache

The Kiowa-Apaches, although always few in number (under five hundred), are unique in being the only Apache group that remained wholly in the Plains after the Comanches had ousted all other Plains Apaches. They were able to achieve this through close alliance with the Kiowa, with whom they established a symbiotic relation while still retaining their own language and tribal identity.

William E. Bittle summarizes what is known of their background in "A Brief History of the Kiowa Apache" [6]. There is no publication on Kiowa-Apache culture as a whole. Nonetheless, a very detailed account of life within the network of kinship is to be found in "Kiowa-Apache Social Organization" [113] by J. Gilbert McAllister, and Patricia Anne Freeman has reported on

Kiowa-Apache child-training in a long article, "Kiowa Apache Concepts and Attitudes toward the Child" [42]. Two good personal histories add dimension to the scant literature on the tribe. Especially interesting is *Dä vé ko* [114], by McAllister, for it covers the life of a medicine man. Jim Whitewolf, A Kiowa-Apache, writes of himself in *Jim Whitewolf* [189].

Comanche

The Comanches are Shoshoneans who, instead of withdrawing westward from the headwaters of the Yellowstone River under pressures from the Blackfoot and other invading tribes, moved south in the eighteenth century to become masters of the extreme southern plains in the mid-nineteenth century. They adapted well to predatory horse nomadism on the Plains but still retained much of their old Shoshonean–Great Basin culture.

A full historical-anthropological account of the Comanches is available in the work by Ernest Wallace and E. Adamson Hoebel, *The Comanches* [182]. Hoebel's monograph *The Political Organization and Law-ways of the Comanche Indians* [60] is the pioneer work in the study of American Indian tribal law systems and reveals the dynamism of dispute settlement among these turbulent people. An excellent biography of the last of the Comanche medicine women, *Sanapia*, by David E. Jones [74], provides a sensitive inside view of Comanche curing and religion. Ralph Linton [98] wrote a handy behavioral summary of Comanche culture, to which the psychoanalyst Abram Kardiner [75] added a psychodynamic interpretation that lends some interesting insights into Comanche tribal character.

ALPHABETICAL LIST AND INDEX

*Denotes items suitable for secondary school students.

Item no.		Essay page no.
[1]	* Baird, W. David. 1972. *The Osage People.* Phoenix: Indian Tribal Series.	(22)
[2]	Bass, Althea. 1966. *The Arapaho Way, A Memoir of an Indian Boyhood.* New York: C. N. Potter, Inc.	(28)
[3]	Beckwith, Martha Warren. 1938. *Mandan-Hidatsa Myths and Ceremonies.* New York: *Memoirs of the American Folklore Society* 32.	(21)
[4]	Bell, Charles N., ed. 1928. *The Journal of Henry Kelsey (1691–1692.).* Winnipeg: Historical and Scientific Society of Manitoba, *Transactions,* n.s., 4.	(15)
[5]	Berthrong, Donald J. 1963. *The Southern Cheyennes.* Norman: University of Oklahoma Press.	(29)
[6]	Bittle, William E. 1971. "A Brief History of the Kiowa Apache." *Papers in Anthropology* 12:1-34.	(43)
[7]	* Bleeker, Sonia. 1962. *The Sioux Indians,*	

Hunters and Warriors of the Plains. New York: William Morrow and Co.   (35)

[8]   Bloomfield, Leonard. 1934. *Plains Cree Texts.* New York: *Publications of the American Ethnological Society* 16.   (41)

[9]   Bolton, Herbert E., ed. 1916. *Spanish Exploration in the Southwest, 1542–1706.* New York: Charles Scribner's Sons.   (15)

[10]   Bonner, Thomas D., ed. 1969. *The Life and Adventures of James P. Beckwourth.* New York: Arno Press. (Reprinted, Lincoln, Neb.: University of Nebraska Press, 1972.)   (32)

[11]   Bowers, Alfred W. 1950. *Mandan Social and Ceremonial Organization.* Chicago: University of Chicago Press.   (20)

[12]   _____. 1965. *Hidatsa Social and Ceremonial Organization.* Washington, D. C.: *Bureau of American Ethnology Bulletin* 194.   (21)

[13] * Brown, Joseph, E. 1953. *The Sacred Pipe: Black Elk's Account of the Seven Rites of the Oglala Sioux.* Norman: University of Oklahoma Press. (Reprinted, Baltimore: Penguin Books, 1971.)   (36)

[14]   Bruner, Edward M. 1961. "Differential Change in the Culture of the Mandan

from 1250 to 1953." In *Perspectives in American Indian Culture Change,* ed. Edward H. Spicer, pp. 187–277. Chicago: University of Chicago Press.   (20)

[15] * Cash, Joseph, H. 1971. *The Sioux People (Rosebud).* Phoenix: Indian Tribal Series.   (35)

[16]   Catlin, George. 1967. *O-Kee-Pa: A Religious Ceremony and Other Customs of the Mandans,* ed. John C. Ewers. New Haven: Yale University Press.   (20)

[17]   ———. 1973. *Letters and Notes on the Manners, Customs, and Conditions of the North American Indians, Written during Eight Years' Travel (1832–1839) amongst the Wildest Tribes of Indians in North America.* 2 vols. New York: Dover Publications. (16, 20)

[18]   Cooper, John M. 1956. *The Gros Ventres of Montana.* Part II. *Religion and Ritual,* ed. Regina Flannery. Washington, D. C.: Catholic University of America Anthropological Series* 16.   (31)

[19]   De Land, Charles E. 1906. *The Aborigines of South Dakota,* ed. Doane Robinson. Pierre: *South Dakota Historical Collections* 3:267–586.   (21)

[20]   Deloria, Ella. 1929. "The Sun Dance of

the Oglala Sioux." *Journal of American Folklore* 42:354–413.   (36)

[21]   Deloria, Vine. 1969. *Custer Died for Your Sins: An Indian Manifesto.* New York: Macmillan.   (37)

[22] * Denig, Edwin T. 1961. *Five Indian Tribes of the Upper Missouri: Sioux, Arikaras, Assiniboines, Crees, Crows,* ed. John C. Ewers. Norman: University of Oklahoma Press.   (17, 35)

[23]   Densmore, Frances. 1918. *Teton Sioux Music.* Washington, D. C.: *Bureau of American Ethnology Bulletin* 61.   (36)

[24]   _____. 1936. *Cheyenne and Arapaho Music.* Los Angeles: *Southwest Museum Papers* 10.   (28)

[25]   Dodge, Richard I. 1877. *The Plains of the Great West and Their Inhabitants, Being a Description of the Plains, Game, Indians, &c. of the Great North American Desert.* New York: G. P. Putnam's Sons. (Reprinted, New York: Archer House, 1959.)   (8)

[26]   Dorsey, George A. 1903. *The Arapaho Sun Dance: The Ceremony of the Offerings Lodge.* Chicago: *Field Columbian Museum Anthropological Series* 4.   (28)

[27]   _____. 1904. *Traditions of the Skidi Paw-nee*. Boston and Washington, D. C.: *American Folklore Society Memoir 8*.   *(26)*

[28]   _____. 1905. *The Cheyenne*. 2 vols. Vol. II: *The Sun Dance*. Chicago: *Field Colum-bian Museum Anthropological Series* 9, no. 2.   (30)

[29]   _____. 1906. *The Pawnee: Mythology*. Washington, D. C.: Carnegie Institution of Washington.   (26)

[30]   Dorsey, George A., and Alfred L. Kroeber. 1903. *Traditions of the Arapaho*. Chicago: *Field Columbian Museum Anthro-pological Series* 5.   (28)

[31]   Dorsey, George A., and James R. Murie. 1940. *Notes on Skidi Pawnee Society*. Chi-cago: *Field Museum of Natural History An-thropological Series* 27:67–119.   (25)

[32]   Driver, Harold E., and James L. Coffin. 1975. *Classification and Development of North American Indian Cultures: A Statisti-cal Analysis of the Driver–Massey Sample*. Philadelphia: *Transactions of the American Philosophical Society*, n.s., 65, pt. 3.   (12)

[33]   Eggan, Fred. 1955. "The Cheyenne and Arapaho Kinship System." In *Social An-thropology of North American Tribes*, ed.

Fred Eggan, pp. 33–95. Chicago: University of Chicago Press. (28)

[34] Elkin, Henry. 1940. "The Northern Arapaho of Wyoming." In *Acculturation in Seven American Indian Tribes,* ed. Ralph Linton, pp. 207–258. New York: Appleton-Century Co. (27)

[35] Erikson, Erik H. 1964. *Childhood and Society.* 2d ed., rev. and enlarged. New York: W. W. Norton and Co. (37)

[36] Ewers, John C. 1955. *The Horse in Blackfoot Indian Culture: With Comparative Materials from Other Western Tribes.* Washington, D. C.: *Bureau of American Ethnology Bulletin* 159. (18, 38)

[37] * _____. 1958. *The Blackfeet: Raiders on the Northwestern Plains.* Norman: University of Oklahoma Press. (38)

[38] _____. 1968. *Indian Life on the Upper Missouri.* Norman: University of Oklahoma Press. (17)

[39] Flannery, Regina. 1953. *The Gros Ventres of Montana.* Part I. *Social Life.* Washington, D. C.: *Catholic University of America Anthropological Series* 15. (31)

[40] Fletcher, Alice C., and Francis La Flesche. 1911. *The Omaha Tribe.* Wash-

ington, D. C.: *Bureau of American Ethnology Annual Report* 27 (1905–06).   (22)

[41]   Fortune, Reo F. 1932. *Omaha Secret Societies*. New York: *Columbia University Contributions to Anthropology* 14.   (22)

[42]   Freeman, Patricia Anne. 1971. "Kiowa Apache Concepts and Attitudes toward the Child." *Papers in Anthropology* 12:90–168.   (44)

[43]   Goldfrank, Esther S. 1945. *Changing Configurations in the Social Organization of a Blackfoot Tribe during the Reserve Period: The Blood of Alberta, Canada*. New York: *American Ethnological Society Monograph* 8.   (39)

[44]   Grinnell, George B. 1889. *Pawnee Hero Stories and Folk-Tales, with Notes on the Origin, Customs and Character of the Pawnee People*. New York: Forest and Stream Publishing Co. (Reprinted, Lincoln: University of Nebraska Press, 1976.)   (26)

[45]   _____. 1892. *Blackfoot Lodge Tales: The Story of a Prairie People*. New York: Charles Scribner's Sons. (Reprinted, Lincoln: University of Nebraska Press, 1962.)   (39)

[46]   _____. 1915. *The Fighting Cheyennes*.

New York: Charles Scribner's Sons. (Reprinted, Norman: University of Oklahoma Press, 1956.) (29)

[47] _____. 1920. *When Buffalo Ran.* New Haven: Yale University Press. (29)

[48] _____. 1923. *The Cheyenne Indians: Their History and Ways of Life.* 2 vols. New Haven: Yale University Press. (Reprinted, Lincoln: University of Nebraska Press, 1972.) (29, 30)

[49] _____. 1926. *By Cheyenne Campfires.* New Haven: Yale University Press. (Reprinted, Lincoln: University of Nebraska Press, 1971.) (29)

[50] Gross, Hugo. 1951. "Mastodons, Mammoths, and Man in North America," ed. Alex D. Krieger. *Bulletin of the Texas Archeological and Paleontological Society* 22:101–131.

[51] Hammond, George P., and Agapito Rey, trans. and eds. 1940. *Narratives of the Coronado Expedition, 1540–1542.* Albuquerque: University of New Mexico Press. (15)

[52] Hanks, Lucien M., and Jane Richardson Hanks. 1950. *Tribe under Trust: A Study of*

the Blackfoot Reserve of Alberta. Toronto: University of Toronto Press.   (39)

[53]   Hanson, James A. 1975. *Metal Weapons, Tools, and Ornaments of the Teton Dakota Indians.* Lincoln: University of Nebraska Press.   (34, 53)

[54]   Harrington, John P. 1928. *Vocabulary of the Kiowa Language.* Washington, D. C.: *Bureau of American Ethnology Bulletin* 84.   (43)

[55]   Hartman, Horst. 1973. *Die Plains- und Prairieindianer Nordamericas.* Berlin: *Veröffentlichungen des Museums für Völker-kunder Berlin,* Neue Folge 22, *Abteilung Americanishe Naturvölker* II.   (6)

[56]   Hassrick, Royal B. 1964. *The Sioux: Life and Customs of a Warrior Society.* Norman: University of Oklahoma Press.   (35)

[57]   Hendry, Anthony. 1907. *York Factory to the Blackfeet Country: The Journal of Anthony Hendry, 1754–55,* ed. Lawrence J. Burpee, *Proceedings and Transactions of the Royal Society of Canada,* 3d ser., 1:307–360.   (15)

[58]   Henry, Alexander, and David Thompson. 1897. *New Light on the Early History of the Greater Northwest, 1799–1814* ed. El-

liott Coues. 3 vols. New York: F. P.
Harper. (16)

[59] Hilger, Inez. 1952. *Arapaho Child Life
and Its Cultural Background.* Washington,
D. C.: *Bureau of American Ethnology Bulletin* 148. (28)

[60] Hoebel, E. Adamson. 1940. *The Political
Organization and Law-ways of the Comanche
Indians. American Anthropological Association Memoir* 54. (44)

[61] _____. 1960. *The Cheyennes: Indians of
the Great Plains.* New York: Holt. (29)

[62] * Holder, Preston. 1970. *The Hoe and the
Horse on the Plains: A Study of Cultural
Development among North American Indians.* Lincoln: University of Nebraska
Press. (17)

[63] Howard, James H. 1965. *The Ponca
Tribe.* Washington, D. C.: *Bureau of American Ethnology Bulletin* 195. (24)

[64] * Hyde, George E. 1937. *Red Cloud's Folk:
A History of the Oglala Sioux.* Norman:
University of Oklahoma Press. (34)

[65] * _____. 1951. *Pawnee Indians.* Denver:
University of Denver Press. (26)

[66]   _____. 1956. *A Sioux Chronicle.* Norman: University of Oklahoma Press.   (37)

[67]   _____. 1959. *Indians of the High Plains: From the Prehistoric Period to the Coming of Europeans.* Norman: University of Oklahoma Press.   (15)

[68]   _____. 1961. *Spotted Tail's Folk: A History of the Brulé Sioux.* Norman: University of Oklahoma Press.   (34)

[69]   Jablow, Joseph. 1951. *The Cheyenne in Plains Indian Trade Relations, 1795–1840.* New York: *American Ethnological Society Monograph* 19.   (17)

[70]   Jenness, Diamond. 1934. *The Indians of Canada,* 2d ed. Ottawa: *National Museum of Canada Bulletin* 65, Anthropological Series 15.   (40)

[71]   Jennings, Jesse D. 1974. *Prehistory of North America,* 2d ed. New York: McGraw-Hill Book Company.   (7, 14)

[72]   Jennings, Jesse D., and Edward Norbeck. 1964. *Prehistoric Man in the New World.* Chicago: University of Chicago Press.   (14)

[73]   Johnson, Elden. 1965. "The Teton Dakota." In Robert F. Spencer, Jesse D.

Jennings, et al., *The Native Americans,* pp.
350–381. New York: Harper and Row.   (35)

[74] * Jones, David E. 1972. *Sanapia: Comanche
Medicine Woman.* New York: Holt, Rinehart and Winston.   (44)

[75]   Kardiner, Abram. 1945. "Analysis of
Comanche Culture." In Abram Kar-
diner, et al., *The Psychological Frontiers of
Society,* pp. 81–100. New York: Columbia University Press.   (45)

[76]   Kennedy, Dan. 1972. *Recollections of an
Assiniboine Chief,* ed. James R. Stevens.
Toronto: McClelland and Stewart.   (40)

[77]   Kennedy, Michael S., ed. 1961. *The As-
siniboines: From the Accounts of the Old Ones
Told to First Boy (James Larpenteur Long).*
Norman: University of Oklahoma Press.   (40)

[78]   Kenner, Charles L. 1969. *A History of
New Mexican–Plains Indian Relations.*
Norman: University of Oklahoma Press.   (15)

[79]   Kroeber, Alfred L. 1902–1907. *The
Arapaho.* New York: *American Museum of
Natural History Bulletin* 18:1–229, 279–
454.   (27)

[80]   _____. 1908. *Ethnology of the Gros Ventre.* New York: *American Museum of Nat-*

ural History Anthropological Papers 1, pt. 5.   (30)

[81]   _____. 1939. *Cultural and Natural Areas of Native North America.* Berkeley: *University of California Publications in American Archaeology and Ethnology* 38.   (10)

[82]   La Barre, Weston. 1970. *The Ghost Dance: Origins of Religion.* Garden City: Doubleday.   (37)

[83]   La Flesche, Francis. 1921. *The Osage Tribe: Rite of the Chiefs; Sayings of the Ancient Men.* Washington, D. C.: *Bureau of American Ethnology Annual Report* 36 (1914–15).   (23)

[84]   _____. 1925. *The Osage Tribe: The Rite of Vigil.* Washington, D. C.: *Bureau of American Ethnology Annual Report* 39 (1917–1918).   (23)

[85]   _____. 1928. *The Osage Tribe: Two Versions of the Child-naming Rite.* Washington, D. C.: *Bureau of American Ethnology Annual Report* 43 (1925–26).   (23)

[86]   _____. 1930. *The Osage Tribe: Rite of the WA-XÓ-BE.* Washington, D. C.: *Bureau of American Ethnology Annual Report* 45 (1927–28).   (23)

[87]   _____. 1939. *War Ceremony and Peace Ceremony of the Osage Indians.* Washing-

ton, D. C.: *Bureau of American Ethnology Bulletin* 101. (23)

[88] Larpenteur, Charles. 1898. *Forty Years a Fur Trader on the Upper Missouri: The Personal Narrative of Charles Larpenteur, 1833–1872,* ed. Elliott Coues. 2 vols. New York: F. P. Harper. (40)

[89] La Vérendrye, Pierre Gaultier de Varennes, Sieur de. 1927. *Journals and Letters of Pierre Gaultier de Varennes de la Vérendrye and His Sons, with the Correspondence between the Governors of Canada and the French Court, Touching the Search for the Western Sea,* ed. Lawrence J. Burpee. Toronto: The Champlain Society. (16, 40)

[90] Lehmer, Donald J. 1971. *Introduction to Middle Missouri Archeology.* Washington, D. C.: *National Park Service Anthropological Papers* 1. (14)

[91] Leonard, Zenas. 1904. *Leonard's Narrative: Adventures of Zenas Leonard, Fur Trader and Trapper, 1831–1836,* ed. W. F. Wagner. Cleveland: The Burrows Brothers Co. (32)

[92] Lesser, Alexander. 1933. *The Pawnee Ghost Dance Hand Game: A Study of Cultural Change.* New York: *Columbia University Contributions to Anthropology* 16. (26)

[93]   Lewis, Meriwether. 1902. *History of the Expedition of Captains Lewis and Clark, 1804–5–6*, ed. James K. Hosmer. 2 vols. Chicago: A. C. McClurg and Co.   (16)

[94]   ———. 1904–1905. *The Original Journals of the Lewis and Clark Expedition, 1804–1806,* ed. Reuben Gold Thwaites. 8 vols. New York: Dodd, Mead and Co.   (16)

[95]   Lewis, Oscar. 1942. *The Effects of White Contact upon Blackfoot Culture, with Especial Reference to the Role of the Fur Trade.* New York: *American Ethnological Society Monograph* 6.   (17, 38)

[96] * Linderman, Frank B. 1930. *American: The Life Story of a Great Indian, Plenty-Coups, Chief of the Crows.* Yonkers-on-Hudson: World Book Co. (Reprinted as *Plenty Coups, Chief of the Crows.* Lincoln: University of Nebraska Press, 1962.)   (33)

[97] * ———. 1932. *Red Mother.* New York: John Day Co. (Reprinted as *Pretty-Shield, Medicine Woman of the Crows.* New York: John Day Co., 1972.)   (33)

[98]   Linton, Ralph. 1945. "The Comanche." In Abram Kardiner, et al., *The Psychological Frontiers of Society,* pp. 47–99. New York: Columbia University Press.   (45)

[99] _____. ed. 1940. *Acculturation in Seven American Indian Tribes*. New York: D. Appleton-Century Co. (27)

[100] Llewellyn, Karl N., and E. Adamson Hoebel. 1941. *The Cheyenne Way: Conflict and Case Law in Primitive Jurisprudence*. Norman: University of Oklahoma Press. (30)

[101] Lowie, Robert H. 1909. *The Assiniboine*. New York: *Museum of Natural History Anthropological Papers* 4, pt. 1. (40)

[102] _____. 1912. *Social Life of the Crow Indians*. New York: *American Museum of Natural History Anthropological Papers* 9, pt. 2. (32)

[103] _____. 1913. *Military Societies of the Crow Indians*. New York: *American Museum of Natural History Anthropological Papers* 11:143–217. (32)

[104] _____. 1915. *The Sun Dance of the Crow Indians*. New York: *American Museum of Natural History Anthropological Papers* 14, pt. 1. (32)

[105] _____. 1918. *Myths and Traditions of the Crow Indians*. New York: *American Museum of Natural History Anthropological Papers* 25, pt. 1. (32)

[106]   _____. 1919. *The Tobacco Society of the Crow Indians.* New York: *American Museum of Natural History Anthropological Papers* 21, pt. 2.   (32)

[107]   _____. 1922. *Crow Indian Art.* New York: *American Museum of Natural History Anthropological Papers* 21, pt. 4.   (31)

[108]   _____. 1922. *The Material Culture of the Crow Indians.* New York: *American Museum of Natural History Anthropological Papers* 21, pt. 3.   (32)

[109]   _____. 1935. *The Crow Indians.* New York: Farrar and Rinehart.   (31)

[110]   _____. 1941. *The Crow Language.* Berkeley: *University of California Publications in American Archaeology and Ethnology* 39, no. 1.   (32)

[111]   *_____. 1963. *Indians of the Plains.* Garden City: The Natural History Press.   (6)

[112]   Lyford, Carrie A. 1940. *Quill and Beadwork of the Western Sioux.* Lawrence, Kansas: Haskell Institute.   (36)

[113]   McAllister, J. Gilbert. 1955. "Kiowa-Apache Social Organization." In *Social Anthropology of North American Tribes,* ed. Fred Eggan, pp. 97–172. Chicago: University of Chicago Press.   (43)

[114] _____. 1970. *Dä vé ko: Kiowa-Apache Medicine Man.* Austin: *Texas Memorial Museum Bulletin* 17.   (44)

[115] McClintock, Walter. 1910. *The Old North Trail; or, Life, Legends and Religion of the Blackfeet Indians.* London: Macmillan and Co. (Reprinted Lincoln: University of Nebraska Press, 1968.)

[116] MacEwan, John W. 1969. *Tatanga Mani: Walking Buffalo of the Stories.* Edmonton: M. G. Hurtig.   (40)

[117] *McFee, Malcolm. 1972. *Modern Blackfeet: Montanans on a Reservation.* New York: Holt, Rinehart and Winston.   (39)

[118] McGee, W J 1897. *The Siouxan Indians: A Preliminary Sketch.* Washington, D. C.: *Bureau of American Ethnology Annual Report* 15 (1893–94).

[119] *McGinnis, Dale K., and Floyd W. Sharrock. 1972. *The Crow People.* Phoenix: Indian Tribal Series.   (32)

[120] Macgowan, Ernest S. 1942. "The Arikara Indians," *Minnesota Archaeologist* 8:83–122.   (21)

[121] Macgregor, Gordon. 1946. *Warriors without Weapons: A Study of the Society and Personality Development of the Pine Ridge*

Sioux. Chicago: University of Chicago Press.   (37)

[122] *Mails, Thomas E. 1972. *The Mystic Warriors of the Plains*. Garden City: Doubleday and Co.   (6)

[123] Mandelbaum, David G. 1940. *The Plains Cree*. New York: *American Museum of Natural History Anthropological Papers* 37, pt. 2.   (41)

[124] *Marquis, Thomas B. 1928. *Memoirs of a White Crow Indian* (Thomas H. Leforge). New York: The Century Co.   (33)

[125] *———. 1931. *A Warrior Who Fought Custer*. Minneapolis: The Midwest Co. (Reprinted as *Wooden Leg: A Warrior Who Fought Custer*. Lincoln: University of Nebraska Press, 1957.)   (30)

[126] *Marriott, Alice L. 1945. *The Ten Grandmothers*. Norman: University of Oklahoma Press.   (42)

[127] *———. 1963. *Saynday's People: The Kiowa Indians and the Stories They Told*. Lincoln: University of Nebraska Press.   (43)

[128] *———. 1968. *Kiowa Years: A Study in Culture Impact*. New York: Macmillan and Co.   (42)

[129] *Mathews, John J. 1932. *Wah' kon-tah: The Osage and the White Man's Road.* Norman: University of Oklahoma Press. (22)

[130] ———. *The Osages: Children of the Middle Waters.* Norman: University of Oklahoma Press. (22)

[131] Matthews, Washington. 1877. *Ethnography and Philology of the Hidatsa Indians.* Washington, D. C.: *United States Geological and Geographical Survey Miscellaneous Publications* 7. (Reprinted New York: Johnson Reprint Co., 1971. (20)

[132] Maximilian Alexander Philipp, Prince of Wied-Neuwied. 1906. *Travels in the Interior of North America, 1832–1834.* In *Early Western Travels,* ed. Reuben Gold Thwaites, vols. 22–24. 32 vols. Cleveland: Arthur H. Clark Co. 1904–1907. (16)

[133] Mayhall, Mildred P. 1971. *The Kiowas.* 2d ed. Norman: University of Oklahoma Press. (41)

[134] Mead, Margaret. 1932. *The Changing Culture of an Indian Tribe.* New York: *Columbia University Contributions to Anthropology* 15. (22)

[135] *Mekeel, Scudder. 1943. "A Short His-

tory of the Teton Dakota." *North Dakota Historical Quarterly* 10:137–205.   (34)

[136] Mirsky, Jeanette. 1937. "The Dakota." In *Cooperation and Competition among Primitive Peoples,* ed. Margaret Mead, pp. 382–427. New York: McGraw-Hill Book Co.   (35)

[137] Mishkin, Bernard. 1940. *Rank and Warfare among the Plains Indians.* New York: *American Ethnological Society* Monograph 3.   (42)

[138] Mooney, James A. 1896. *The Ghost Dance Religion and the Sioux Outbreak of 1890.* Washington, D. C.: *Bureau of American Ethnology Annual Report* 14 (1892–93), pt. 2.   (37)

[139] _____. 1898. *Calendar History of the Kiowa Indians.* Washington, D. C.: *Bureau of American Ethnology Annual Report* 17 (1895–96), pt. 1.   (42)

[140] Murdock, George P., and Timothy J. O'Leary. 1975. *Ethnographic Bibliography of North America,* 4th ed. Vol. 5. *Plains and Southwest.* New Haven: Human Relations Area Files Press.   (1, 21)

[141] Murie, James R. 1914. *Pawnee Indian Societies.* New York: *American Museum of*

Natural History Anthropological Papers 11, pt. 7. (25)

[142] *Nabokov, Peter. 1967. *Two Leggings: The Making of a Crow Warrior.* New York: Thomas Y. Crowell and Co. (33)

[143] *Neihardt, John G. 1932. *Black Elk Speaks: Being the Life Story of a Holy Man of the Ogalala Sioux.* New York: William Morrow and Co. (36)

[144] *Nye, Wilbur S. 1962. *Bad Medicine and Good: Tales of the Kiowas.* Norman: University of Oklahoma Press. (43)

[145] Oliver, Symmes C. 1962. *Ecology and Cultural Continuity as Contributing Factors in the Social Organization of the Plains Indians.* Berkeley: *University of California Publications in American Archaeology and Ethnology* 48, no. 1. (7)

[146] *Oswalt, Wendell H. 1966. *This Land Was Theirs: A Study of the North American Indian.* New York: John Wiley and Sons. (25)

[147] Paige, Harry W. 1970. *Songs of the Teton Sioux.* Los Angeles: Westernlore Press. (36)

[148] Parsons, Elsie C. 1929. *Kiowa Tales.* New York: *American Folklore Society Memoir* 22. (43)

[149] Powell, Peter J. 1969. *Sweet Medicine:*

The Continuing Role of the Sacred Arrows, the Sun Dance, and the Sacred Buffalo Hat in Northern Cheyenne History. 2 vols. Norman: University of Oklahoma Press.   (30)

[150] Richardson, Jane. 1940. *Law and Status among the Kiowa Indians.* New York: *American Ethnological Society Monograph* 1.   (42)

[151] Richardson, Rupert N. 1933. *The Comanche Barrier to South Plains Settlement: A Century and a Half of Savage Resistance to the Advancing White Frontier.* Glendale: Arthur H. Clark Co.   (15)

[152] Robinson, Doane. 1904. *A History of the Dakota or Sioux Indians from Their Earliest Traditions and First Contact with White Men to the Final Settlement of the Last of Them upon Reservations and the Consequent Abandonment of the Old Tribal Life.* Pierre: *South Dakota Historical Collections* 2. (Reprinted Minneapolis: Ross and Haines, 1956.)   (34)

[153] Rodnick, David. 1936. "The Fort Belknap Assiniboine of Montana." Philadelphia: Ph.D. diss., University of Pennsylvania.   (40)

[154] *Sandoz, Mari. 1961. *These Were the Sioux.* New York: Hastings House. (Reprinted, New York: Dell Publishing Co., 1967.)   (35)

[155] *Schultz, James W. 1916. *Blackfeet Tales of Glacier National Park*. Boston: Houghton Mifflin Co. (39)

[156] *———. 1962. *Blackfeet and Buffalo: Memories of Life among the Indians*, ed. Keith C. Seele. Norman: University of Oklahoma Press. (39)

[157] Secoy, Frank R. 1953. *Changing Military Patterns on the Great Plains (17th Century through Early 19th Century)*. Locust Valley, N.Y.: *American Ethnological Society Monograph* 21. (15, 17)

[158] Skinner, Alanson B. 1914. *Political Organization, Cults and Ceremonies of the Plains–Ojibway and Plains–Cree Indians*. New York: *American Museum of Natural History Anthropological Papers* 11, pt. 6. (41)

[159] ———. 1926. *Ethnology of the Ioway Indians*. Milwaukee: *Public Museum of the City of Milwaukee Bulletin* 5, no. 4. (24)

[160] Spencer, Robert F., Jesse D. Jennings, et al. 1965. *The Native Americans*. New York: Harper and Row. (35)

[161] *Standing Bear, Luther. 1928. *My People the Sioux*. Boston: Houghton Mifflin Co. (36)

[162] *———. 1933. *Land of the Spotted Eagle*. Boston: Houghton Mifflin Co. (36)

[163] *Stands in Timber, John, and Margot Liberty, with the assistance of Robert M. Utley. 1967. *Cheyenne Memories*. New Haven: Yale University Press. (29)

[164] Strong, William D. 1933. "The Plains Culture Area in the Light of Archaeology." *American Anthropologist* 35: 271–287. (13, 18)

[165] _____. 1935. *An Introduction to Nebraska Archaeology*. Washington, D. C.: *Smithsonian Miscellaneous Collections* 93, no. 10.

[166] Tabeau, Pierre Antoine. 1939. *Tabeau's Narrative of Loisel's Expedition to the Upper Missouri,* ed. Annie H. Abel. Norman: University of Oklahoma Press. (21)

[167] *Trenholm, Virginia C. 1970. *The Arapahoes, Our People*. Norman: University of Oklahoma Press. (28)

[168] *Underhill, Ruth Murray. 1953. *Red Man's America: A History of Indians in the United States*. Chicago: University of Chicago Press. (6)

United States. Indian Claims Commission. 1974. *American Indian Ethnohistory Series, Plains Indians,* comp. and ed. David Agee Horr. New York: Garland Publishing Co.

[169]   _____. *Arapaho–Cheyenne Indians.*   (28)

[170]   _____. *Blackfeet Indians.*   (38)

[171]   _____. *Crow Indians.*   (32)

[172]   _____. *Kiowa–Commanche Indians.* 2 vols.   (43)

[173]   _____. *Omaha Indians.*   (22)

[174]   _____. *Osage Indians.* 5 vols.   (23)

[175]   _____. *Oto and Missouri Indians.*   (24)

[176]   _____. *Pawnee and Kansa (Kaw) Indians.*   (25)

[177]   _____. *Ponca Indians.*   (24)

[178]   _____. *Sioux Indians.* 4 vols.   (34)

[179]   Utley, Robert M. 1963. *The Last Days of the Sioux Nation.* New Haven: Yale University Press.   (37)

[180]   Vestal, Paul A., and Richard E. Schultes. 1939. *The Economic Botany of the Kiowa Indians as It Relates to the History of Their Tribe.* Cambridge, Mass.: Botanical Museum.   (42)

[181]   Walker, J. R. 1917. *The Sun Dance and Other Ceremonies of the Ogalala Division of the Teton Dakota.* New York: *American Museum of Natural History Anthropological Papers* 16, pt. 2.   (36)

[182]   *Wallace, Ernest, and E. Adamson

Hoebel. 1952. *The Comanches: Lords of the South Plains*. Norman: University of Oklahoma Press. (44)

[183] Webb, Walter P. 1931. *The Great Plains*. Boston: Ginn and Co. (8)

[184] Wedel, Waldo R. 1936. *An Introduction to Pawnee Archeology*. Washington, D. C.: *Bureau of American Ethnology Bulletin* 112. (26)

[185] _____. 1961. *Prehistoric Man on the Great Plains*. Norman: University of Oklahoma Press. (11, 12, 14)

[186] _____. 1964. "The Great Plains." In *Prehistoric Man in the New World,* ed. Jesse D. Jennings and Edward Norbeck, pp. 193–220. Chicago: University of Chicago Press. (14)

[187] Weltfish, Gene. 1965. *The Lost Universe, with a Closing Chapter on The Universe Regained*. New York: Basic Books. (26)

[188] Wendorf, Fred, Alex D. Krieger, Claude C. Albritton, and T. D. Stewart. 1955. *The Midland Discovery: A Report on the Pleistocene Human Remains from Midland, Texas*. Austin: University of Texas Press. (12)

[189] Whitewolf, Jim. 1969. *Jim Whitewolf: The Life of a Kiowa Apache Indian,* ed. Charles S. Brant. New York: Dover Publications. (44)

[190] Whitman, William. 1932. *The Oto.* New York: *Columbia University Contributions to Anthropology* 28. (24)

Wied-Neuwied, Maximilian Alexander Philipp, Price of. *See* [132] Maximilian Alexander Philipp, Prince of Wied-Neuwied.

[191] Will, George F., and George E. Hyde. 1917. *Corn among the Indians of the Upper Missouri.* St. Louis: W. H. Miner Co. (Reprinted, Lincoln: University of Nebraska Press, 1964 and 1976.) (21)

[192] Will, George F., and Herbert J. Spinden. 1906. *The Mandans: A Study of Their Culture, Archaeology and Language.* Cambridge, Mass.: *Papers of the Peabody Museum of American Archaeology and Ethnology, Harvard University* 3, no. 4. (20)

[193] Wilson, Gilbert L. 1917. *Agriculture of the Hidatsa Indians.* Minneapolis: *University of Minnesota Studies in the Social Sciences* 9. (21)

[194] _____. 1924. *The Horse and Dog in Hidatsa Culture.* New York: *American Museum of Natural History Anthropological Papers* 15, pt. 2. (21)

[195] Wissler, Clark. 1905. "Decorative Art of the Sioux Indians," *Bulletin of the Ameri-*

can Museum of Natural History 18:231–277.   (36)

[196] _____. 1910. *The Material Culture of the Blackfoot Indians.* New York: *American Museum of Natural History Anthropological Papers* 5, pt. 1.   (39)

[197] _____. 1912. *Ceremonial Bundles of the Blackfoot Indians.* New York: *American Museum of Natural History Anthropological Papers* 7, pt. 2.   (39)

[198] _____. 1912. *Societies and Ceremonial Associations in the Oglala Division of the Teton–Dakota.* New York: *American Museum of Natural History Anthropological Papers* 11, pt. 1.   (36)

[199] _____. 1913. *Societies and Dance Associations of the Blackfoot Indians.* New York: *American Museum of Natural History Anthropological Papers* 11, pt. 4.   (39)

[200] _____. 1914. "The Influence of the Horse in the Development of Plains Culture." *American Anthropologist* 16:1–25.   (17)

[201] _____. 1917. *The American Indian: An Introduction to the Anthropology of the New World.* New York: D. C. McMurtrie.   (8)

[202] _____. 1918. *The Sun Dance of the Black-*

foot Indians. New York: *American Museum of Natural History Anthropological Papers* 16, pt. 3. (39)

[203] Wissler, Clark, and D. C. Duvall. 1908. *Mythology of the Blackfoot Indians.* New York: *American Museum of Natural History Anthropological Papers* 2, pt. 1. (39)

[204] Wood, W. Raymond. 1967. *An Interpretation of Mandan Culture History.* Washington, D. C.: *Bureau of American Ethnology Bulletin* 198. (20)

[205] _____. 1971. *Biesterfeldt: A Post-Contact Coalescent Site on the North-Eastern Plains.* Washington, D. C.: *Smithsonian Contributions to Anthropology* 15. (28)

The Newberry Library
Center for the History of the American Indian
Director: Francis Jennings

Established in 1972 by the Newberry Library, in conjunction with the Committee on Institutional Cooperation of eleven midwestern universities, the Center makes the resources of one of America's foremost research libraries in the Humanities available to those interested in improving the quality and effectiveness of teaching American Indian history. The Newberry's collections include some 100,000 volumes on the history of the American Indian and offer specialized resources for studying historical aspects of Indian-White relations and Indian linguistics. The Center also assists Native Americans engaged in writing tribal histories and developing educational materials.

ADVISORY COMMITTEE

Chairman: D'Arcy McNickle